Ramkumar Ramaswamy is co-founder of Performance Engineering Associates (www.pea-online.com), a consulting firm that specializes in scientific, quantitative techniques for performance engineering of IT systems. He received his PhD in Operations Research from the Indian Institute of Management and has nearly two decades of IT industry experience, playing strategic and not-so-strategic advisor to several large corporations worldwide. Inspired by Edward Lear's *The Book of Nonsense*, this is his maiden foray into limericks.

Also by Ramkumar Ramaswamy

The Art and Technology of Software Engineering

THE PERFORMANCE ENGINEERING BOOK OF NONSENSE

A Tale of the Tardy, in Limericks

RAMKUMAR RAMASWAMY

Illustrated by Rajeshwari Ganesan

ISBN: 1449997538

EAN-13: 9781449997533

Published by:

Performance Engineering Associates

www.pea-online.com

For Kuttan and Kunju

An Introduction

Welcome, gentle reader, to this characteristic tale

About IT applications which on performance fail.

The limericks here

Embody a message clear:

It's science that counts, if your applications must scale.

Why 'nonsense,' besides the inspiration from Lear?

Though the science has been around for many a year,

I am usually bemused

That the science is unused

By practitioners wedded to 'intuition' and trial and error.

What's with this science that practitioners don't touch?

Is it arcane or convoluted, involving relativity and such?

The truth, beyond belief,

Is fit for comic relief:

It's barely high school math; now is that too much?

The Project Is Won

There was once a CEO in a faraway land

Who gave her customers the best on hand.

But their apps weren't slick,

Nor particularly quick;

'Twas time they moved on to technology grand.

She called her CIO James without wasting time –

Her IT shop was known to be truly sublime.

"Let's cut the crap,

And build an app

That runs with sub-second response time."

Thought James, "This project will be my pride,"

And called upon his trusted vendors worldwide.

ISO? CMM? They had it all,

And were at his beck and call;

Courting the project as they would a ravishing bride.

Proposals were floated, aggressive bids did they pitch.

Negotiations were hectic; who was gonna get rich?

You guessed who won:

The proposal weighing a ton.

Sales was happy; but would Delivery need a witch?

Project manager Jay was assigned, a PMO floated;

"We'll create absolute customer ecstasy," he gloated.

Schedules were tight

(No fun without a fight);

Was this to be a large project, or was it merely bloated?

These are weighty proposals

Chapter Endnotes

If you happen to be a reader not well-versed in IT,

But picked up my attempt at poetry in curiosity,

You may encounter a word

That appears fit for a nerd;

Use these endnotes so you may enjoy the poetry.

Requirements Are Captured

The requirements team, as always, planted the seed;

They got to work brandishing their performance creed.

Many a question did they ask

Of stakeholders trained in their task;

And made pretty pictures in CASE tools best of breed.

"What's your need, how many seconds this page?"

They asked, in honest efforts to requirements gauge.

"Make it lean –

A second is the mean –

And oh, the maximum is two, else face users' rage."

System history was rich; transaction logs they did exhume;

"Peak hour matters most, that's when users fume."

But the intra-peak burst,

As governed by Hurst,

And long-tailed traffic, they missed; would this cause gloom?

Users were profiled, their potential numbers counted;

Fingers crossed as the virtual user budgets mounted.

James paused to think;

He couldn't afford to blink;

This was his pride: the money wouldn't have him daunted.

"A performance PoC," said Jay, "is what we need."

It was their best practice, he proudly decreed;

"A little code,

A scaled-down load,

And subsequently with full development we'll proceed."

It's the long-tailed
Koch-ness monster

Chapter Endnotes

The **Hurst factor** and fractal **self-similarity**

Describe bursty Web traffic especially when heavy.

A **CASE tool** is meant to aid

Programmers otherwise afraid

To build a system that's out of touch with reality.

A **long-tailed** distribution, unlike the classic **Poisson**

Is one in which outliers show unexpected domination.

Virtual users, as you guessed,

Mimic real ones during a test;

Effective use, though, requires science – not fashion.

Servers Are Sized

A spanking new application it was going to be;

New boxes they'd need, with the greatest TPC.

With clusters in a farm;

"A few extra – no harm –

Will take care of things," thought James with glee.

Mike, the capacity planner, was around as well,

Making headroom projections as best as he could tell.

"It's a Web-based app

And we have CPUs on tap;"

But what would the wickedness of self-similarity spell?

Above all they had consultants of a Big Four

Flesh out the plans in the dark suits they wore.

They brought strategic vision

And much handwaving precision;

Placing proprietary wisdom, it seemed, at the fore.

Curiously enough, the capacity planning blokes

Did not use specs from the requirements folks.

With the weaknesses in the plot,

Would it matter? Perhaps not;

Call it an antipattern if you will, or better just a joke.

Finally the plan was baselined, for all to admire and use.

"We'll add value," pips Jay, "can we do some reviews?"

So validate they did,

Without blowing any lid;

Their intelligent comments merely lengthened the fuse.

Their handwaving is a best practice

Chapter Endnotes

TPC is a popular benchmark for server hardware;

Some think more of it makes your application a hare.

Methods commonly in use,

Though science they abuse,

Are called **anti-patterns**; oppose them but with care!

The System Is Built

The architects were well-versed in technologies galore:

Databases, application servers, tools from the Big Four.

"Performance? No sweat,"

Each said, "you'll dance, we bet."

Styles and patterns were chosen; but what was in store?

The programmers arrived, all young and bright,

Ready to design code, recode, if through the night.

The first iteration was easy:

After all, just a PoC;

Did you really think the PoC would create a fright?

The PoC happened as planned, quite convincing at that,

With test tools purring silently, churning 3D graphs, not flat!

And so signoffs were got;

But there's a twist to the plot –

How were the results extrapolated? Did you think of that?

Now the programmers were commissioned at last

To build and test their code – and fast.

They toiled like asses,

Profiling their classes,

As they had done with all their projects past.

Functional enhancements kept happening too;

"Let's squeeze all the juice," was the CEO's view.

More pages, more stuff;

Said Jay, off the cuff,

"Performance? We'll handle that in a week or two."

I'm told profiling isn't donkeywork

Chapter Endnotes

A Proof-of-Concept (**PoC**) is a comforting notion;

But its results are useless without scientific extrapolation.

Profiling of software

Uses tools that declare

Portions of code that involve the most computation.

The System Is Tested

The performance testers arrived; 'twas finally their day:

Armies of script-writers, each interviewed by Jay.

Test case design

To himself James did assign;

"Leadership is key," thought he, "I need to show them the way."

The test environment was set up: Mike got it done;

Bought the latest boxes – it was time to have fun!

Sizing the boxes right?

Seemed intuitive all right

To Mike; he had experience – projects by the ton.

Virtual users were set up to mimic each and every one:

Marketing, administration, and customers needing to be won.

A thousand there were,

Hosted on many a server;

That they actually needed only a few score, realized none.

Scenarios were designed, and how ideas flew!

Intense debate on ramp ups and – gosh – ramp downs too.

Think times must randomize

To emulate users, thought the wise;

We're so glad they didn't use viruses to mimic their flu!

Some bottlenecks were found, so testing looked good;

"Are we certifying deployment?" not one did brood.

Attacked were the hot spots

By the profiling bigots;

But not much thought went into requests queued.

They need the tests to be realistic

Chapter Endnotes

A large server farm is where an application deploys;

The **test environment** is somewhat smaller in size.

Ramp up is how users spawn;

The converse is **ramp down**;

That they aren't fit for debate would seem a surprise.

Load any system and some **bottleneck** you'll spot;

Change the load and it's a different one you've got!

This classic test conundrum

Would seem but humdrum

With some knowledge of **queues**, even if self-taught.

The System Is Deployed

As dawn broke on a bright December Five,

The spanking new system slithered into Live.

Said all, "Man this is cool,"

With a collective drool;

And they made plans for a grand New Year Jive.

At Ten AM, the going was still strong,

Though some noticed the login took a bit long.

"No cause for any alarm;

Just a rendezvous point – no harm."

And they waited for more customers to come along.

Peak hour arrived and veritably changed the world,

Or so it seemed: visitors found the site go cold.

Whether you clicked there or here,

Pages took forever to appear;

"Darn," said Mike, "but the utilizations were as foretold!"

"Teething troubles," said Jay, "tweaking is a must-do."

So tuning experts came in with their microscopic view.

Each tuned their bit;

Their hourly rates? Worth it!

Now we wonder what happened to the top-down view.

The rest of the story is painful – I'll keep it brief;

Troubles stayed, customers went; the project came to grief.

James was fired, Jay was too;

To the system users bid adieu.

Mike was promoted to give the IT 'strategy' some beef.

They say it's squarely about tuning

Chapter Endnotes

Utilization, as the name quite simply suggests,

Measures how busy a server on average gets.

Tuning sure feels good

When you're under the hood;

Sans the big picture though, would you place any bets?

In Conclusion

As with many a real case, the tale must end forlorn;

'Cause 'Best Practice' in PE is but an oxymoron.

I hope you itch

To make a method switch:

From cowboy stuff to scientific rigor to rely on.

If you're serious about business workload capture,

Statistical workload modeling is a must, to be sure.

Poisson's often the way to go;

And self-similar for Web 2.0;

Do beware – modeling from scratch is a tempting lure.

When it comes to users, while they know their job,

'Maximum response times' will get your bottom on a hob.

Percentiles are the key:

Not one but many!

Watch how you tie them to SLAs, lest you lose your job.

Capacity planning may seem like it needs sorcery,

Till you realize that the workload model's the key.

Intuition isn't without flaw:

You need Little's Law

And beyond; you must embrace queuing theory.

Performance testing isn't art; science it certainly is;

But shoot darts empirically, and you'll obviously miss.

With tools no matter how good,

You need theory under the hood;

And that ignorance, my friend, cannot be deemed bliss.

Chapter Endnotes

A gripping branch of mathematics, **queuing theory**,

Models servers with traffic that keeps them busy.

Little's Law, a simple rule,

Is a truly universal tool;

Comprehending which, remarkably, requires no degree.

www.ingramcontent.com/pod-product-compliance
Lightning Source LLC
Chambersburg PA
CBHW041147050326
40689CB00001B/521